To

From

You're the Best!

Compiled by Suzanne Siegel Zenkel

Illustrated by Jenny Faw

PETER PAUPER PRESS, INC
WHITE PLAINS · NEW YORK

YOU'RE
THE BEST!

Be yourself. Who else is better qualified?

FRANK J. GIBLIN II

Do what you know best;
if you're a runner, run, if
you're a bell, ring.

IGNAS BERNSTEIN

If you do the best you can, you will find, nine times out of ten, that you have done as well as or better than anyone else.

WILLIAM FEATHER

That's it, baby! When you got it, flaunt it! Flaunt it!

MEL BROOKS,
The Producers

If you want a place in the
sun, you've got to put up
with a few blisters.

ABIGAIL VAN BUREN

Success to me is having
ten honeydew melons
and eating only the top
half of each one.

BARBRA STREISAND

A man is a success if he
gets up in the morning
and goes to bed at night
and in between does
what he wants to do.

BOB DYLAN

The only real risk is the
risk of thinking too small.

FRANCES MOORE LAPPE

I like thinking big. I
always have. To me it's
very simple: if you're
going to be thinking
anyway, you might as
well think big.

DONALD TRUMP

Success is not so much
achievement as achiev-
ing. Refuse to join the
cautious crowd that plays
not to lose; play to win.

DAVID J. MAHONEY

Behind every man who
achieves success
Stand a mother, a wife,
and the IRS.

ETHEL JACOBSON

Success didn't spoil me;
I've always been
insufferable.

FRAN LEBOWITZ

When in doubt, wear
red.

BILL BLASS

It is better to be looked
over than overlooked.

MAE WEST

Perseverance is a great
element of success. If
you only knock long
enough and loud enough
at the gate, you are sure
to wake up somebody.

HENRY WADSWORTH
LONGFELLOW

What really matters is
what you do with what
you have.

SHIRLEY LORD

It's better to be a lion for a day than a sheep all your life.

SISTER KENNY

I was the best I ever had.

WOODY ALLEN

If I only had a little humility, I would be perfect.

TED TURNER

When someone does
something good,
applaud! You will make
two people happy.

SAMUEL GOLDWYN

It takes twenty years to make an overnight success.

EDDIE CANTOR

It is a funny thing about
life; if you refuse to
accept anything but the
best, you very often get it.

W. SOMERSET MAUGHAM

My mother drew a distinction between achievement and success. She said that *achievement is the knowledge that you have studied and worked hard and done the best that is in you. Success is being*

praised by others, and that's nice, too, but not as important or satisfying. Always aim for achievement and forget about success.

HELEN HAYES

If you think you can, you can. And if you think you can't, you're right.

MARY KAY ASH

We are what we believe
we are.

BENJAMIN N. CARDOZO

I've never sought success in order to get fame and money; it's the talent and the passion that count in success.

INGRID BERGMAN

To be successful, the
first thing to do is fall in
love with your work.

SISTER MARY LAURETTA

Find out what you like
doing best and get some-
one to pay you for doing
it.

KATHERINE WHITEHORN

There is only one success—to be able to spend your life in your own way.

CHRISTOPHER MORLEY

They can do all because
they think they can.

VIRGIL

Success can make you go one of two ways. It can make you a prima donna, or it can smooth the edges, take away the insecurities, let the nice things come out.

BARBARA WALTERS

A show of envy is an
insult to oneself.

YEVGENY YEVTUSHENKO

Every individual has a place to fill in the world and is important in some respect whether he chooses to be so or not.

NATHANIEL HAWTHORNE

I must admit that I
personally measure
success in terms of the
contributions an indi-
vidual makes to her or
his fellow human beings.

MARGARET MEAD

We don't know who we are until we see what we can do.

MARTHA GRIMES

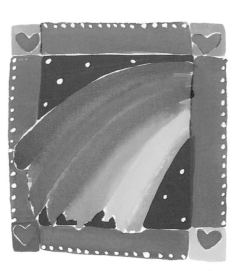

You are the product of
your own brainstorm.

ROSEMARY
KONNER STEINBAUM

Talent is a flame. Genius
is a fire.

BERN WILLIAMS

Until you try, you don't know what you can't do.

HENRY JAMES

You always pass failure
on the way to success.

MICKEY ROONEY

Neither birth nor sex
forms a limit to genius.

CHARLOTTE BRONTË

Victory is not won in miles but in inches. Win a little now, hold your ground, and later win a little more.

LOUIS L'AMOUR

Success breeds
confidence.

BERYL MARKHAM

Just go out there and do
what you've got to do.

MARTINA NAVRATILOVA

Success is that old A B C—ability, breaks and courage.

CHARLES LUCKMAN

Everybody has their ups
and downs so I decided
to have mine between
good and great.

DANIEL HOOGTRERP

Genius is one per cent
inspiration and ninety-
nine per cent perspiration.

THOMAS A. EDISON

There are no secrets to success. It is the result of preparation, hard work, learning from failure.

GEN. COLIN L. POWELL

There aren't any great men. There are just great challenges that ordinary men like you and me are forced by circumstances to meet.

WILLIAM F. HALSEY

The one who removes a mountain begins by carrying away small stones.

Success is not the result of spontaneous combustion. You must set yourself on fire.

REGGIE LEACH

If you really want some-
thing you can figure out
how to make it happen.

CHER

How can they say my life isn't a success? Have I not for more than sixty years got enough to eat and escaped being eaten?

LOGAN PEARSALL SMITH

There never has been
one like me before, and
there never will be one
like me again.

HOWARD COSELL

Self-confidence is the
first requisite to great
undertakings.

SAMUEL JOHNSON

The best is good enough.

GERMAN PROVERB

Some are born great,
some achieve greatness,
and some have greatness
thrust upon 'em.

WILLIAM SHAKESPEARE

My greatest strength is that I have no weak-nesses.

JOHN McENROE

A man cannot be comfortable without his own approval.

MARK TWAIN

Taking joy in life is a
woman's best cosmetic.

ROSALIND RUSSELL

There's only one corner
of the universe you can
be certain of improving
and that's your own self.

ALDOUS HUXLEY

The greatest success
is successful self-
acceptance.

BEN SWEET

I've finally stopped
running away from
myself. Who else is there
better to be?

GOLDIE HAWN

It's not true that nice guys finish last. Nice guys are winners before the game even starts.

ADDISON WALKER

I am not a has-been. I'm
a will be.

LAUREN BACALL

Shoot for the moon.
Even if you miss it you
will land among the
stars.

LES BROWN

You're the best!